VEGAN DESSERTS BAKERY

More than 50 Exciting Quick and Easy New Vegan Recipes for Cookies and Pies, Cupcakes and Cakes--and More!

Daniel Smith

Table of Contents

HEALTHY VEGAN DESSERTS RECIPES 1

MORE THAN 50 EXCITING QUICK AND EASY NEW VEGAN RECIPES FOR COOKIES AND PIES, CUPCAKES AND CAKES-- AND MORE! 1

DANIEL SMITH 1

TABLE OF CONTENTS 3

INTRODUCTION 9

    Coconut Cake with Chocolate Ganache .. **Errore. Il segnalibro non è definito.**
    Orange Cranberry Cake............................ **Errore. Il segnalibro non è definito.**
    Marbled Banana Bread............................. **Errore. Il segnalibro non è definito.**
    Chocolate Mint Cake................................. **Errore. Il segnalibro non è definito.**
    Red Wine Chocolate Cake .... **Errore. Il segnalibro non è definito.**
    Coconut and Orange Cake .... **Errore. Il segnalibro non è definito.**
    Applesauce Spice Cake.............................. **Errore. Il segnalibro non è definito.**
    Red Velvet Beet Cake .... **Errore. Il segnalibro non è definito.**
    Simple Chocolate Cake............................. **Errore. Il segnalibro non è definito.**
    Coconut Bread .... **Errore. Il segnalibro non è definito.**
    Ginger and Applesauce Cake .... **Errore. Il segnalibro non è definito.**
    Walnut Carrot Cake .... **Errore. Il segnalibro non è definito.**
    Strawberry Cake.. **Errore. Il segnalibro non è definito.**
    Banana Blueberry Cake............................ **Errore. Il segnalibro non è definito.**
    Cinnamon Swirl Cake .... **Errore. Il segnalibro non è definito.**
    Banana Coffee Cake.................................. **Errore. Il segnalibro non è definito.**
    Date and Walnut Cake.............................. **Errore. Il segnalibro non è definito.**
    Chocolate Zucchini Cake .... **Errore. Il segnalibro non è definito.**
    Cranberry Carrot Cake .... **Errore. Il segnalibro non è definito.**
    Orange Poppy Seed Cake .... **Errore. Il segnalibro non è definito.**
    Lemon Poppy Seed Cake .... **Errore. Il segnalibro non è definito.**
    Chocolate Banana Carrot Cake .... **Errore. Il segnalibro non è definito.**
    Coconut Cake with Caramel Sauce.......... **Errore. Il segnalibro non è definito.**
    Cardamom Carrot Cake .... **Errore. Il segnalibro non è definito.**

Mandarin Cake .... **Errore. Il segnalibro non è definito.**
Chocolate Orange Cake .... **Errore. Il segnalibro non è definito.**
Peach Upside-Down Cake .... **Errore. Il segnalibro non è definito.**
Pineapple Upside-Down Cake .... **Errore. Il segnalibro non è definito.**
Raspberry Chocolate Cake .... **Errore. Il segnalibro non è definito.**
Cherry, Walnut and Banana Cake .... **Errore. Il segnalibro non è definito.**
Cherry Snack Cake .... **Errore. Il segnalibro non è definito.**
Chocolate Zucchini Mud Cake .... **Errore. Il segnalibro non è definito.**
Vegan Basic Vanilla Cake .... **Errore. Il segnalibro non è definito.**
Olive Oil Rosemary Semolina Cake .... **Errore. Il segnalibro non è definito.**
Apfelkuchen .... **Errore. Il segnalibro non è definito.**
Blueberry Chocolate Cake .... **Errore. Il segnalibro non è definito.**
Blueberry Whole Wheat Muffins .... **Errore. Il segnalibro non è definito.**
Chocolate Chip Cookie Dough Muffins.... **Errore. Il segnalibro non è definito.**
Banana and Sunflower Muffins .... **Errore. Il segnalibro non è definito.**
Fudgy Chocolate Muffins .... **Errore. Il segnalibro non è definito.**
Tropical Coconut Muffins .... **Errore. Il segnalibro non è definito.**
Melon Muffins .... **Errore. Il segnalibro non è definito.**
Multigrain Muffins .... **Errore. Il segnalibro non è definito.**
Almond Cranberry Muffins .... **Errore. Il segnalibro non è definito.**
Ginger and Banana Muffins .... **Errore. Il segnalibro non è definito.**
Plum Muffins .... **Errore. Il segnalibro non è definito.**
Blackberry Corn Muffins .... **Errore. Il segnalibro non è definito.**
Sweet Potato Ginger Muffins .... **Errore. Il segnalibro non è definito.**
Quinoa Raspberry Muffins .... **Errore. Il segnalibro non è definito.**
Applesauce Cardamom Muffins .... **Errore. Il segnalibro non è definito.**

© Copyright 2021 by Daniel Smith - All rights reserved.

The following Book is reproduced below with the goal of providing information that is as accurate and reliable as possible. Regardless, purchasing this Book can be seen as consent to the fact that both the publisher and the author of this book are in no way experts on the topics discussed within and that any recommendations or suggestions that are made herein are for entertainment purposes only. Professionals should be consulted as needed prior to undertaking any of the action endorsed herein.

This declaration is deemed fair and valid by both the American Bar Association and the Committee of Publishers Association and is legally binding throughout the United States.

Furthermore, the transmission, duplication, or reproduction of any of the following work including specific information will be considered an illegal act irrespective of if it is done electronically or in print. This extends to creating a secondary or tertiary copy of the work or a recorded copy and is only allowed with the express written consent from the Publisher. All additional right reserved.

The information in the following pages is broadly considered a truthful and accurate account of facts and as such, any inattention, use, or misuse of the information in question by the reader will render any resulting actions solely under their purview. There are no scenarios in which the publisher or the original author of this work can be in any fashion deemed liable for any hardship or damages that may befall them after undertaking information described herein.

Additionally, the information in the following pages is intended only for informational purposes and should thus be thought of as universal. As befitting its nature, it is presented without assurance regarding its prolonged validity or interim quality. Trademarks that are mentioned are done without written consent and can in no way be considered an endorsement from the trademark holder.

Introduction

Congratulations on your smart and brilliant move in stepping forward to the prospect of a wonderful and harmonious life with nature! Not everyone chooses to make the biggest and most important change and, for that, I applaud you! Now you are going to be exposed to the world of delicious and creative recipes—101 wonderful vegan desserts. Unlike many prejudices that suggest that vegans don't have desserts at all, this book is going to surprise you!! You will learn that there are dozens of wonderful and nutritious ways to end a meal in a harmonious and healthy way.

Chocolate and Goji Berry Muffins

The Goji berries have a high content of antioxidants and fiber so adding them to your diet is very beneficial to your health. These muffins are moist and dense, almost fudgy-like in consistency, and absolutely delicious.

Servings: 12 muffins

Ingredients:
1 cup whole wheat flour
1 teaspoon baking soda
1 teaspoon baking powder
1 teaspoon cinnamon powder
1 pinch salt
¼ cup cocoa powder
1 cup almond milk
¼ cup coconut oil
1 teaspoon vanilla extract
¼ cup agave syrup
¼ cup Goji berries, chopped

Directions:

1. In a bowl, combine the whole wheat flour, baking soda, baking powder, cinnamon, and cocoa powder, as well as a pinch of salt.
2. Stir in the almond milk, coconut oil, vanilla extract, and agave syrup.
3. Give it a good mix then fold in the Goji berries.
4. Transfer the batter to your muffin pan lined with muffin papers and bake in a preheated oven at 350°F for 20-30 minutes or until fragrant and golden brown.
5. Remove the pan from the oven and allow the muffins to completely cool before serving.

Walnut and Chia Muffins

These muffins are a bomb of fiber and that makes them perfect for your morning meals. Enjoy them along with a glass of orange juice and you're set to have a great day ahead.

Servings: 12 muffins

Ingredients:

1½ cups almond milk

½ cup applesauce

1 teaspoon apple cider vinegar

1½ cups all-purpose flour

½ cup whole wheat flour

1 teaspoon baking soda

2 tablespoons chia seeds

½ teaspoon cinnamon powder

1 cup walnuts, chopped

1 pinch salt

Directions:

1. Mix the almond milk with the vinegar and applesauce.
2. Stir in the flours, followed by the baking soda, chia seeds, cinnamon powder, and salt.
3. Fold in the walnuts then spoon the batter into your muffin cups.
4. Bake the muffins in a preheated oven at 350°F for 20-30 minutes or until fragrant and golden brown.
5. Allow the muffins to cool before serving.

Pumpkin Millet Muffins

When making vegan muffins, no other kind of ingredients other than plain flour and millet maybe used. However, millet is a great choice as it not only brings taste and texture to these muffins, but also fiber and other nutrients too.

Servings: 16 muffins

Ingredients:
2 tablespoons ground flax seeds
4 tablespoons water
½ cup coconut oil
½ cup agave syrup
1 cup coconut milk
1½ cups pumpkin purée
½ cup rolled oats
1 cup millet
1½ cups whole wheat flour
1 teaspoon baking soda
1 teaspoon baking powder
1 pinch salt
1 teaspoon cinnamon powder

Directions:

1. In a bowl, combine the ground flax seeds with the water.
2. Add the coconut oil, followed by the agave syrup, coconut milk, and pumpkin purée and mix well
3. Incorporate the rolled oats, millet, flour, baking powder, salt, baking soda, and cinnamon.
4. Give it a good mix then transfer the batter to your muffin cups lined with muffin papers and bake in a preheated oven at 350°F for 20-30 minutes or until fragrant and golden brown.
5. Allow the muffins to cool in the pan before serving or storing.

Gluten-Free Cupcakes

If you have a gluten allergy or intolerance, these muffins are perfect for you. They are glutenfree but this recipe does not sacrifice on taste at all. Instead, it combines healthy and nutritious ingredients to create moist, dense, and delicious muffins to help with your sweet cravings.

Servings: 12 muffins

Ingredients:
2 tablespoons ground flax seeds
4 tablespoons cold water
1½ cups pumpkin purée
¼ cup agave syrup
¼ cup sunflower oil
1 teaspoon vanilla extract
½ cup sorghum flour
½ cup rice flour
½ cup oat flour
½ cup arrowroot powder
1 teaspoon baking soda
1 pinch salt
¼ teaspoon ground cardamom
¼ teaspoon ground cloves
½ teaspoon cinnamon powder

Directions:

1. Mix the flax seeds with the cold water, then add the pumpkin purée, agave syrup, oil, and vanilla.
2. Mix well then stir in the flours, arrowroot powder, baking soda, salt, andspices.
3. Mix very well then spoon the batter into your muffin pan lined with muffin papers.
4. Bake the muffins in a preheated oven at 350°F for 20-30 minutes until they rise and turn golden brown.
5. Remove the pan from the oven when ready and allow the muffins to cool in the pan.

Peanut Butter Muffins

Everyone loves peanut butter, but it can also be used to create delicious desserts or snacks, not just to spread on toast. Its flavor infuses the batter so the final muffins are rich and flavorful.

Servings: 10-12 muffins

Ingredients:
1½ cups all-purpose flour
1 cup rolled oats
¼ cup cocoa powder
1 pinch salt
1 pinch nutmeg
½ cup agave syrup
½ cup peanut butter
1 cup almond milk

Directions:

1. Mix the peanut butter with the agave syrup.
2. Add the almond milk then stir in the flour, oats, cocoa powder, salt, and nutmeg.
3. Give it a good mix then spoon the batter into your muffin pan lined with muffin papers.
4. Bake in a preheated oven at 350°F for 20-25 minutes or until golden brown.
5. Remove the pan from the oven and allow the muffins to cool before serving.

Vanilla Muffins

These muffins show you that complicated flavors are great, but nothing compares to vanilla. It may be the most used aroma, but it definitely has a lot to offer and these muffins prove it.

Servings: 16 muffins

Ingredients:

2 ½ cups all-purpose flour

1 teaspoon baking soda

1 teaspoon baking powder

1 pinch salt

½ cup agave syrup

2 cups coconut milk

½ cup water

1 teaspoon vinegar

1 tablespoon vanilla extract

½ cup coconut oil

1 vanilla pod, split lengthwise

Directions:

1. Mix the flour with the baking soda, baking powder and salt. Set aside.
2. In a different bowl, combine the agave syrup with the coconut milk, water, vinegar, vanilla extract, coconut oil, and the seeds from the vanilla pod.
3. Pour this mixture over the dry ingredients and mix really well.
4. Spoon the batter into your muffin pans and bake in a preheated oven at 350°F for 20-30 minutes until the muffins turn slightly golden brown and fragrant.
5. Allow the muffins to cool in the pan before serving.

Simple Chocolate Cookies

Chocolate cookies are loved by everyone, but this particular recipe yields some crisp, flavorful and amazing cookies that can be stored for a long period of time.

Yields: 2 dozen

Ingredients:

1 cup whole wheat flour

1 cup golden raisins

1/2 cup rolled oats

2/3 cup brown sugar

2 tablespoons cocoa powder

4 tablespoons coconut oil

1/4 cup water

1 pinch of salt

Directions:

1. In a bowl, mix the flour with raisins, oats, sugar, cocoa powder and oil.

2. Stir in the water and mix well. If the dough is too dry, add more water, spoon by spoon, until the dough becomes easy to work with.

3. Wet your hands and form small dough balls.

4. Arrange them all on a baking tray lined with baking paper and bake in a preheated oven at 350F for 10-15 minutes.

5. Remove from oven and let them cool in the pan. Transfer to a serving plate.

Banana Breakfast Cookies

Banana cookies, just like breads or cakes, are moist and slightly chewy so if you are a fan of these types of cookies, you will love these.

Servings: 4-6 dozen

Ingredients:
2/3 cup rolled oats
2 ripe bananas, mashed
1/4 cup coconut oil
4 tablespoons agave syrup
1 cup mixed dried fruits, chopped
2/3 cup dark chocolate chip cookies
2/3 cup sliced almonds
2 tablespoons flax seeds, ground
4 tablespoons water
1 teaspoon baking soda
1 pinch of salt

Directions:

1. Mix the flax seeds with water and set aside.

2. In a bowl, mix together the bananas, dark chocolate chip, coconut oil and the agave syrup.

3. Stir in the rolled oats, chopped dried fruits, sliced almonds, flax seeds, baking soda and a pinch of salt. Mix until very well combined.

4. Drop spoonfuls of dough into a pan lined with baking paper.

5. Bake the cookies in a preheated oven at 350F for 20 minutes. Cool in the pan then store in an airtight container until serving.

Chocolate Chip Cookies

A touch of chocolate and some simple cookies turn into a real delight to enjoy in your spoil moments. They are crisp and delicious.

Yields: 2 dozen

Ingredients:

4 tablespoons coconut butter or oil

2/3 cup sugar

1 teaspoon vanilla extract

2 tablespoons almond or coconut milk

1 cup whole wheat flour

1/2 cup almond meal

1 teaspoon baking powder

1/2 teaspoon baking soda

1/3 cup dark chocolate chips

1/3 cup walnuts or other nuts, toasted

1 pinch of salt

Directions:

1. Put the butter and sugar in the bowl of a mixer and whip until creamy and light. Add the vanilla and almond milk and mix to combine well.

2. Stir in the flour then the almond meal, baking soda and baking powder, as well as a pinch of salt. Fold in the chocolate chip cookies and nuts.

3. Take spoonfuls of batter and put them on a baking tray lined with baking paper.

4. Bake the cookies in a preheated oven at 350F for 10-15 minutes.

5. Let them cool in the pan before transferring into an airtight container.

Oatmeal and Chocolate Chip Cookies

Oats and chocolate are a dream come true in the land of healthy eating, especially if you are a chocoholic and can't go a day without a bit of chocolate. These cookies are healthy and nutritious so go ahead and make them.

Yields: 3 dozen

Ingredients:

1 cup almond butter, softened
2/3 cup sugar
2 tablespoons flax seeds, ground
4 tablespoons water
1 teaspoon baking powder
1/2 teaspoon baking soda
1 teaspoon vanilla extract
1 2/3 cups all purpose flour
1/2 cup rolled oats
1/2 cup chocolate chips
1 pinch of salt

Directions:

1. In a small bowl, combine the ground flax seeds with water and set aside to soak.

2. In another bowl, mix the sugar with the butter until creamy and fluffy.

3. Stir in the flax seeds then vanilla. Add the flour, rolled oats, baking soda and baking powder, as well as a pinch of salt, and give it a good mix.

4. Fold in the chocolate chips. Drop spoonfuls of batter into the prepared baking pans and bake in a preheated oven at 350F for 15-20 minutes.

5. Store in an airtight container for up to 2 weeks.

Peanut Butter Cookies

Many people like peanut butter, but not many use it in desserts. However, I highly recommend these cookies just because they emphasize the taste of the peanut butter like no other dessert does.

Yields: 3 dozen

Ingredients:

1/2 cup peanut butter

1/2 cup applesauce

1 cup peanut flour (finely ground peanuts)

1/2 cup whole wheat flour

2 tablespoons flax seeds, ground

4 tablespoons water

1/2 cup sugar

1 pinch of salt

1 teaspoon baking powder

1/4 teaspoon baking soda

Directions:

1. In a small bowl or cup, combine the flax seeds with water and set aside to soak.

2. In a bowl, mix the peanut butter, applesauce, soaked flax seeds, sugar and a pinch of salt. Mix with a hand mixer on low speed until well blended.

3. Stir in the flours mixed with baking powder and baking soda.

4. Take spoonfuls of batter and form small balls. Arrange all of them on baking trays lined with baking paper then, using a fork, press them down slightly, making sure each has a mark from the spoon.

5. Bake in a preheated oven at 350 for 15-17 minutes or until fragrant and slightly golden brown. Store in an airtight container for 1-2 weeks.

Banana Maple Oatmeal Cookies

Bananas, maple syrup and oatmeal sounds like a great combination for breakfast, but you can also use those ingredients for dessert, making some delicious and healthy cookies to enjoy in the morning or in the afternoon, whenever you feel like having a snack.

Yields: 3 dozen

Ingredients:

1 1/4 cup rolled oats

1 cup whole wheat flour

1 teaspoon baking soda

1/2 teaspoon baking powder

1 teaspoon cinnamon

1 tablespoon flax seeds, ground

2 tablespoons water

1/2 cup maple syrup

1 ripe banana, mashed

1/2 cup golden raisins

1 teaspoon lemon juice

1 pinch of salt

Directions:

1. In a bowl, mix the flax seeds with water and set aside to soak.

2. In another bowl, mix together the rolled oats, flour, baking powder and soda, 1 pinch of salt and cinnamon, as well as the raisins.

3. Stir in the maple syrup, flax seeds, banana and lemon juice. Mix until well blended, then drop spoonfuls of batter onto your baking pans, lined with parchment paper.

4. Bake the cookies in a preheated oven at 375F for 10-12 minutes until the edges are slightly brown. Cool in the pan then transfer to an airtight container to store.

Tofu Pumpkin Cookies

Tofu is rather mild and doesn't have a strong, distinctive taste. Its saltiness works great with the pumpkin, creating a delicious contrast to enjoy.

Yields: 3 dozen

Ingredients:
1/3 cup whole wheat flour
3/4 cup all purpose white flour
1/2 cup rolled oats
1 teaspoon baking soda
1 teaspoon cinnamon
1/2 teaspoon ground ginger
1 pinch of nutmeg
1/2 cup agave syrup
3/4 cup canned pumpkin puree
6 oz firm tofu, well crumbled
1 teaspoon vanilla extract

Directions:

1. In a bowl, mix together the flours, oats, baking soda, ginger, cinnamon, nutmeg and a pinch of salt.

2. Stir in the agave syrup, pumpkin puree, crumbled tofu and vanilla extract. Mix until well blended.

3. Drop spoonfuls of batter onto your prepared pans (lined with parchment paper) then bake in a preheated oven at 375F for 15-20 minutes.

4. When done, let them cool in the pan then transfer them into an airtight container to store until serving.

Tofu Coconut Cookies

Tofu and coconut have a similar texture so these cookies are consistent and delicious. Plus, they only contain a few easy to find ingredients.

Yields: 3 dozen

Ingredients:
1/2 cup sweetened coconut flakes
1 1/4 cup all purpose flour
1/2 teaspoon baking soda
1/2 cup sugar
8 oz firm tofu, blended until ground
1 teaspoon vanilla extract
5 tablespoons water
2 tablespoons sugar

Directions:

1. In a bowl, mix the coconut, flour, baking soda and sugar. Add the crumbled tofu, vanilla extract and water and stir well. If the dough is hard to mix, add 2 additional tablespoons of water.

2. Form small balls and arrange each one on your prepared pans (lined with parchment paper).

3. Bake in a preheated oven at 375F for 15-20 minutes or until slightly golden brown.

Vanilla Almond Cookies

Vanilla is the most common flavor, but we all still love it and we can't imagine a dessert without a bit of vanilla. But in these cookies, the vanilla is the star and the cookies are delicious and very fragrant.

Yields: 4 dozen

Ingredients:

1 cup almond meal
2 cups whole wheat flour
1/2 cup all purpose flour
1 cup coconut oil, melted
1/4 cup water
3 teaspoons vanilla extract
1 pinch of salt
1 cup powdered sugar

Directions:

1. In a bowl, mix together the flours with a pinch of salt and the almond meal.

2. Stir in the coconut oil and water then add the vanilla extract.

3. Refrigerate the dough for 1 hour then form small dough balls. Arrange all of them on baking trays lined with baking paper.

4. Bake in a preheated oven at 375F for 10-15 minutes. Remove them from the oven and roll all of them in powdered sugar while still warm.

Pumpkin Gingerbread Cookies

Pumpkin and ginger come together in these cookies to create a dessert that is able to awaken your taste buds and send them to heaven.

Yields: 5 dozen

Ingredients:
3 1/4 cups all purpose flour
1 teaspoon baking soda
1/2 teaspoon baking powder
3/4 cup sugar
1/3 cup coconut oil
1/4 cup canned pumpkin puree
1/4 cup maple syrup
1/2 cup molasses
1 teaspoon vanilla extract
1 teaspoon cinnamon
1 pinch of nutmeg
1 pinch of salt

Directions:

1. In a bowl, mix the coconut oil with the sugar then stir in the pumpkin puree, molasses, maple syrup and spices, as well as a pinch of salt. Add the flour, baking soda and baking powder, and mix well. The dough will be fairly thick and sticky.

2. Refrigerate for 1 hour then roll the dough on a well floured surface. It should be 1/2cm thick. Using a cookie cutter, cut the desired shapes.

3. Arrange all of them on baking trays lined with baking paper and bake them in a preheated oven at 350F for 15-20 minutes. Let them cool in the pan then transfer to an airtight container to store.

Shortbread Cookies

This recipe is a basic one and it yields some crisp and crunchy cookies. The recipe is also very versatile and you can add a bunch of other ingredients to it, such as chocolate chips or dried fruits.

Yields: 2 dozen

Ingredients:

1 3/4 cups all purpose flour
2 tablespoons rice flour
1 cup almond butter
1/2 cup sugar
1 teaspoon vanilla extract
1/2 teaspoon lemon zest
1 pinch of salt

Directions:

1. In a bowl, combine the all purpose flour with the rice flour.

2. In another bowl, mix well the almond butter with a hand mixer until fluffy and light. Add the sugar and mix well.

3. Stir in the vanilla and lemon zest and then incorporate the flours. Refrigerate the dough for 1 hour.

4. Flour your working surface well then roll the dough in a 1/4 inch thick sheet. Using a cookie cutter, cut your desired shapes. Arrange all the cookies on a baking tray lined with parchment paper.

5. Bake the cookies in a preheated oven at 350F for 10-15 minutes or until slightly golden on the edges.

6. Let them cool in the pan then transfer to an airtight container to store until serving. They can be decorated with any glaze you want, from chocolate to royal icing.

Maple Walnut Cookies

Walnut cookies are amazing because they taste like fall. This particular recipe may take some time to make, but the final result is well worth it.

Yields: 4 dozen

Ingredients:
3/4 cup maple syrup
2 tablespoons flax seeds, ground
4 tablespoons water
1 cup sugar
1 cup almond butter
1 teaspoon cinnamon
1/4 cup honey
1 teaspoon vanilla extract
1 pinch of salt
1/2 cup walnuts, chopped
1/2 cup golden raisins
2 cups whole wheat flour
2/3 cup all purpose flour
2 2/3 cups rolled oats
1 cup soy flour
1 teaspoon baking powder

Directions:

1. In a small cup or glass, mix the ground flax seeds with water and let them soak for 5 minutes.

2. In a large bowl, mix the butter, sugar, maple syrup, honey, cinnamon, vanilla and salt. Stir in the flax seeds then add the walnuts and raisins. Mix in the flours and baking powder.

3. Knead the dough a couple of times. Form small dough balls and arrange all of them on baking trays lined with parchment paper.

4. Bake in a preheated oven at 350F for 20-25 minutes or until slightly golden brown and fragrant.

5. Store in an airtight container until serving.

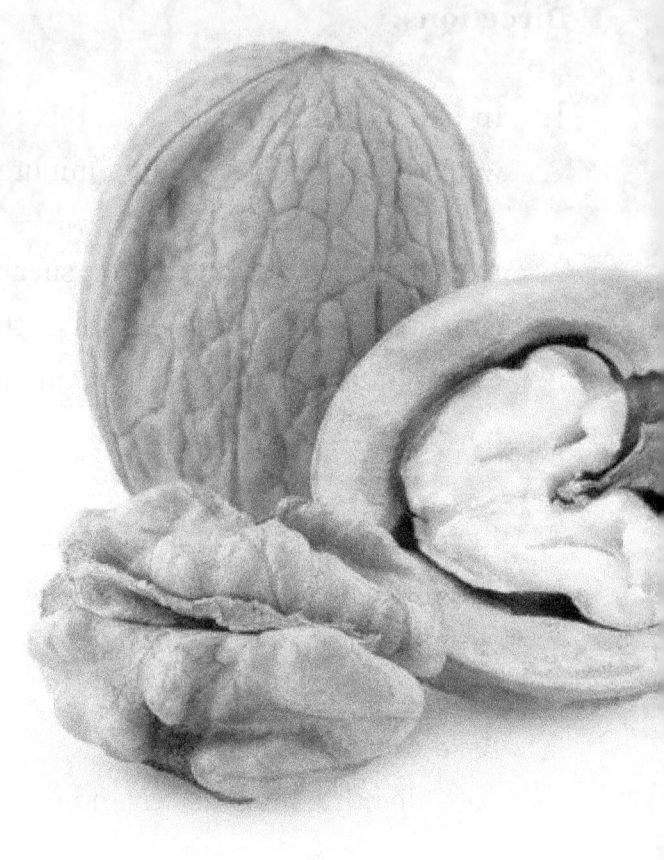

Chocolate Cherry Cookies

Crisp and fragrant, these cookies will impress any diner or guest with their strong chocolate flavor. Chocolate pairs wonderfully with cakes anyway.

Yields: 4 dozen

Ingredients:
2 tablespoons flax seeds, ground
4 tablespoons water
2 cups sugar
1 cup almond butter, melted
1/2 cup brown rice syrup
1 teaspoon vanilla extract
1/2 teaspoon almond extract
1/2 cup dried cherries
1/2 cup dark chocolate chips
1 cup cocoa powder
1 1/2 cups whole wheat flour
1 cup soy flour
1 1/2 teaspoons baking powder
1/2 teaspoon baking soda
1 pinch of salt

Directions:

1. In a small bowl, mix the ground flax seeds with water and let them soak for 5 minutes.

2. In another bowl, mix the melted butter, sugar, brown rice syrup, vanilla, a pinch of salt and almond extract. Stir in the flax seeds then the cherries and chocolate chips.

3. In a separate bowl, mix well the flours, cocoa powder, baking powder and baking soda.

4. Combine the three mixtures in one bowl and give it a good mix. The dough might be very thick, so you can knead it a couple of times with your hands to make sure the ingredients are well incorporated.

5. Form small dough balls and arrange them all on baking trays lined with baking paper.

6. Bake in a preheated oven at 350F for 20-25 minutes.

7. When chilled, store them in an airtight container.

Orange Cashew Cookies

Don't you love orange flavor? Even if you are not a huge fan, these cookies are still worth making because you will get to experience a whole new range of flavors and, who knows, you may actually love it.

Yields: 6 dozen

Ingredients:
1/2 cup maple syrup
3/4 cup brown rice syrup
2/3 cup coconut oil
1 teaspoon vanilla extract
1 cup cashews, coarsely chopped
2 cups barley flour
2 cups oat flour
2 tablespoons orange zest
1 teaspoon cinnamon
1 teaspoon baking soda
1 pinch of salt

Directions:

1. In a bowl, mix together the maple syrup with brown rice syrup, coconut oil and vanilla extract. Add the chopped cashews then stir in the flours, orange zest, cinnamon, baking soda and a pinch of salt. Mix well then form small dough balls. Arrange all of them on a baking tray lined with parchment paper.

2. Bake the cookies in a preheated oven at 350F for 15-20 minutes.

3. Store them in an airtight container until serving.

Cranberry and Pistachio Cookies

Pistachios are special because compared with other nuts they have a richer taste, although not too strong. So, paired with cranberries, they create some amazing, delightful cookies.

Yields: 3 dozen

Ingredients:
1 1/2 cups all purpose flour
1 1/2 cups whole wheat flour
1 teaspoon baking powder
1 teaspoon baking soda
1 teaspoon orange zest
1 cup sugar
1/4 cup orange juice
1/2 cup coconut milk
4 tablespoons coconut oil
1 teaspoon vanilla extract
2 tablespoons cornstarch
1 pinch of salt
1 cup dried cranberries
1 cup shelled pistachios, chopped

Directions:

1. In a bowl, mix together the flours, baking powder and baking soda, as well as a pinch of salt. In another bowl, mix the coconut oil with sugar, coconut milk and orange juice and zest, as well as vanilla extract and cornstarch.

2. Beat with a hand mixer for 5 minutes then stir in the dry ingredients. Fold in the dried cranberries and pistachios.

3. Form small dough balls and arrange all of them on baking trays lined with baking paper.

4. Bake the cookies in a preheated oven at 350F for 15-20 minutes. Let them cool in the pan then transfer them into an airtight container to store.

Apple Cookies

Apples are very common and easy to find so using them in all sort of desserts is a good idea. Plus, they are flavorful and, when baked, they turn very soft and creamy.

Yields: 4 dozen

Ingredients:
2 cups quick oats
1 cup whole wheat flour
1/2 cup all purpose flour
1 teaspoon baking powder
1 teaspoon cinnamon
1/2 teaspoon ground cloves
1/4 cup coconut oil 3/4 cup sugar
1/2 cup applesauce
1 cup almond milk
1 teaspoon vanilla extract
1/2 teaspoon salt
1 cup grated apples
1/4 cup golden raisins

Directions:

1. In a bowl, mix together the flours with the quick oats, baking powder, baking soda, cinnamon, ground cloves and a pinch of salt. Stir in the milk, applesauce, vanilla, sugar and coconut oil. Fold in the grated apples and raisins.

2. Drop spoonfuls of this dough onto the prepared pans (lined with parchment paper).

3. Bake the cookies in a preheated oven at 350F for 15 minutes until slightly golden brown and fragrant.

4. Store in an airtight container until serving.

Double Chocolate Cookies

If simple chocolate cookies aren't enough to satisfy your craving, here is a recipe that uses a double dose of chocolate, creating some delicious, amazing cookies.

Yields: 2 dozen

Ingredients:
2 cups all purpose flour
3/4 cup cocoa powder
1 teaspoon baking powder
1/4 cup coconut oil
1/2 cup maple syrup
3 tablespoons flax seeds, ground
1/2 cup coconut milk
1 teaspoon almond extract
1 cup dark chocolate chips
1/2 cup chopped walnuts
1/4 cup dried cherries
1 pinch of salt

Directions:

1. In a bowl, mix together the flour, cocoa powder, baking powder and a pinch of salt. In another bowl, mix together the coconut oil, milk, flax seeds and almond extract.

2. Combine the two mixtures and mix well. Fold in the chocolate chips, dried cherries and chopped walnuts.

3. Line your baking trays with baking paper and drop spoonfuls of batter onto each tray.

4. Bake in a preheated oven at 375F for 15-20 minutes or until fragrant.

5. Store in an airtight container until serving.

Hazelnut Cookies

Hazelnuts and cocoa are the main ingredients of these cookies so the final result is absolutely delicious and flavorful, with a silky texture, yet crunchy and interesting.

Yields: 2 dozen

Ingredients:
3/4 cup almond milk
2 tablespoons ground flax seeds
1/2 cup sugar
1/2 cup coconut oil
1 teaspoon vanilla extract
1 1/2 cup whole wheat flour
1/2 cup rolled oats
1/3 cup cocoa powder
2 teaspoons baking powder
1 cup hazelnuts, coarsely chopped
1 pinch of salt

Directions:

1. In a large bowl, mix the milk and flax seeds and let them soak for 1 minute.

2. Stir in the sugar, oil and vanilla extract, as well as a pinch of salt. Sift in the flour, cocoa powder and baking powder. Give it a good mix then fold in the chopped hazelnuts.

3. Drop spoonfuls of batter onto your greased pans and bake in a preheated oven at 350F for 15-20 minutes.

4. When done, remove from oven and let them cool in the pan. When chilled, transfer to an airtight container to store.

Barley Flour Vegan Cookies

Barley is not a common ingredient in desserts, but don't let that put you off. It's very healthy and tasty and it will surprise you in a most pleasant way.

Yields: 3 dozen

Ingredients:
1/2 cup peanut butter
1/2 cup almond butter
2/3 cup brown sugar
1/3 cup white sugar
1 teaspoon vanilla extract
2 tablespoons ground flax seeds mixed with 4 tablespoons of water
1 1/2 cup barley flour
1 teaspoon baking soda
1 cup rolled oats
1/2 cup Rice Krispies
1/2 cup walnuts, chopped
1/2 cup golden raisins
1 pinch of salt

Directions:

1. In a bowl, mix together the peanut butter, almond butter and sugar until fluffy and creamy.

2. Stir in the flax seeds and vanilla then add the barley flour, baking soda and a pinch of salt. Fold in the rolled oats, Rice Krispies, walnuts and raisins.

3. Spoon this batter onto baking trays lined with parchment paper.

4. Bake the cookies in a preheated oven at 350F for 20-25 minutes or until slightly golden brown.

5. Store in an airtight container until serving.

Spiced Oatmeal Cookies

Oatmeal and lots of spices make these cookies a real delight for your morning meal, next to a glass of warm milk or a cup of tea.

Yields: 3 dozen

Ingredients:
1/2 cup unsweetened applesauce
1 tablespoon ground flax seeds
1/3 cup brown sugar
1 teaspoon vanilla extract
3/4 cup spelt flour
1 teaspoon baking soda
1/2 teaspoon baking powder
1/2 teaspoon cinnamon
1/2 teaspoon ground ginger
1 pinch of nutmeg
1/2 teaspoon ground cloves
1 1/3 cups rolled oats
1/2 cup golden raisins
1 pinch of salt

Directions:

1. In a large bowl, mix together the applesauce and flax seeds and allow to sit for 5 minutes. Add the sugar and salt, mixing well, then stir in the vanilla.

2. In another bowl, sift the flour with baking soda, baking powder, cinnamon, ginger, nutmeg and ground cloves then add the rolled oats.

3. Combine the two mixtures then fold in the golden raisins.

4. Drop spoonfuls of this batter onto the greased baking trays.

5. Bake in a preheated oven at 350F for 15-20 minutes or until slightly golden brown on the edges.

6. Store in an airtight container until serving.

Simple Banana and Oatmeal Cookies

Simple recipes are sometimes the best and these cookies make no exception. With just two ingredients, these cookies are moist and as healthy as can be.

Yields: 1 dozen

Ingredients:
2 large bananas, mashed
1 cup rolled oats

Directions:

1. Mix the two ingredients together then drop spoonfuls of the final dough onto a baking tray lined with parchment paper.

2. Bake in a preheated oven at 375F for 10-15 minutes or until golden brown and fragrant. If you wish to, you can add other ingredients too, such as chopped walnuts, raisins, chocolate chips and so on.

Pumpkin Molasses Cookies

Pumpkin and spices make these cookies a real delight and fall treat.

Yields: 2 dozen

Ingredients:
1 cup pumpkin puree
1 cup raw sugar
1/2 cup coconut oil
1/4 cup molasses
1 teaspoon vanilla extract
1 cup whole wheat flour
1/2 cup tapioca flour
1/2 cup potato starch
1 teaspoon cinnamon
1 teaspoon baking soda
1 teaspoon ground cloves
1 pinch of salt

Directions:

1. In a bowl, mix the pumpkin puree with the sugar, coconut oil, molasses and vanilla.

2. Stir in the flours, starch, cinnamon, cloves, salt and baking soda. Mix well.

3. Drop spoonfuls of this batter onto a baking tray lined with parchment paper then bake in a preheated oven at 375F for 15-20 minutes or until golden brown and fragrant.

Coconut and Blueberry Ice Cream

Coconut ice cream is very creamy and silky and has a strong flavor that every coconut lover will enjoy.

Servings: 2-4 dishes

Ingredients:
1/2 cup shredded coconut
1/2 teaspoon fresh, grated ginger
2 cups coconut milk
1 teaspoon lemon juice
3/4 cup fresh blueberries

Directions:

1. In a bowl, crush the blueberries with a fork then stir in the lemon juice. Add the ginger, shredded coconut and coconut milk then pour this mixture into the container of your ice cream maker and churn according to manufacturer's instructions.

2. When done, transfer to an airtight container and store in the freezer until serving.

Coconut Pistachio Ice Cream

The great thing about this ice cream, apart from its taste, is its pretty green color which makes it more appealing. In terms of flavor, the final result will exceed any expectations.

Servings: 2-4 dishes

Ingredients:
1 1/2 cups coconut milk
1/2 cup coconut cream
1/4 cup pistachio paste
2 tablespoons raw sugar
1/4 cup chopped pistachios

Directions:

1. Mix the coconut milk with the coconut cream, pistachio paste and sugar.

2. Pour the mixture into your ice cream maker and churn according to the instructions of you machine. A few minutes before it is finished, throw in the chopped pistachio.

3. Serve right away or store in an airtight container in the freezer until needed.

Simple Coconut Ice Cream

With just a few ingredients, you can create a delicious and amazing ice cream that will prove to you that simplicity is better than tons of ingredients and a complicated way of mixing them.

Servings: 2-4 dishes

Ingredients:
1/2 cup sugar
1 1/2 cups coconut milk
1/2 cup cream of coconut
1 teaspoon vanilla extract

Directions:

1. Mix well all the ingredients in a bowl then pour the mixture into your ice cream maker and freeze according to your manufacturer's instructions.

2. When done, transfer to an airtight container and store in the freezer for as long as it takes.

Salted Caramel Ice Cream

As weird as it may sound, salted caramel is absolutely delicious so don't avoid it. Plus, this ice cream is vegan and healthier than other store bought versions.

Servings: 4-6 dishes

Ingredients:
1 1/2 cups coconut milk
1 1/2 cups almond milk
3/4 cup brown sugar
1 teaspoon vanilla extract
2 tablespoons coconut oil
1/2 teaspoon salt

Directions:

1. In a small saucepan, melt the sugar. When melted, add the coconut oil then stir in the coconut milk and salt.

2. Keep on heat until smooth then let it cool.

3. Stir in the almond milk and vanilla then pour the mixture into your ice cream maker and freeze according to manufacturer's instructions.

Avocado Coconut Ice Cream

Avocado is great, not only for savory foods, but also for desserts, and this ice cream is a perfect example of how avocado works in desserts, creating a delicious ice cream for your summer days.

Servings: 2-4 dishes

Ingredients:
2 ripe avocados
1 cup coconut milk
1/2 cup cream of coconut
3/4 cup sugar
1/4 cup shredded coconut

Directions:

1. Peel the avocados and put the flesh into a blender, together with the rest of the ingredients.

2. Pulse until smooth then pour the mixture into the container of an ice cream maker and churn according to manufacturer's instructions.

3. Store in an airtight container in the freezer for as long as it takes.

Spiced Pumpkin Ice Cream

Pumpkin can be used in ice cream, too; in fact, it tastes better than many other ice cream recipes. The pumpkin puree adds a lot of creaminess while the spices add a bit of kick that you will simply love.

Servings: 4-6 dishes

Ingredients:
1 1/2 cups coconut milk
1 1/2 cups canned pumpkin puree
1/2 cup sugar
1 teaspoon cinnamon
1 pinch of nutmeg
1/2 teaspoon ground cloves
1 teaspoon vanilla extract
1/2 teaspoon ground ginger

Directions:

1. In a bowl, mix the coconut milk with the pumpkin puree and sugar then stir in the spices.

2. Pour this mixture into your ice cream maker and freeze according to manufacturer's instructions.

3. Transfer to an airtight container and store in the freezer.

Peanut Butter Ice Cream

Peanut butter is not just for sandwiches, it's also for ice cream. This particular recipe only uses a few ingredients, but the final result will surprise you with how good it tastes.

Servings: 2-4 dishes

Ingredients:
2 cups full fat coconut milk
1/2 cup sugar
2/3 cups peanut butter
2 tablespoons maple syrup

Directions:

1. In a bowl, mix the peanut butter with the sugar and coconut milk then pour into your ice cream maker.

2. Churn according to the instructions provided by your machine's producer then transfer to an airtight container to store in the freezer.

3. Serve in dessert bowls, drizzled with maple syrup.

Mango Ice Cream

If you like tropical flavors, this ice cream will be familiar as the aroma is strong and the texture is silky.

Servings: 2-4 dishes

Ingredients:
1 1/2 cups coconut milk
1/2 cup sugar
1 teaspoon lime juice
1 large mango, peeled and diced
1/2 teaspoon vanilla extract

Directions:

1. Put all the ingredients into a blender and pulse until well blended.

2. Pour the mixture into an ice cream maker and freeze according to manufacturer's instructions.

3. Scoop into an airtight container in order to store in the freezer.

Cinnamon Ice Cream

Cinnamon has a strong aroma, but paired with coconut it yields a delicious ice cream that can cool you off during those hot summer days or be a nice treat during fall or winter if you enjoy ice cream at that time of year, too.

Servings: 2-4 dishes

Ingredients:
3 cups full fat coconut milk
1/2 cup sugar
1 teaspoon vanilla extract
1 teaspoon cinnamon

Directions:

1. Mix well all the ingredients in a bowl then pour the mixture into your ice cream maker and churn according to manufacturer's instructions.

2. When done, transfer to an airtight container and freeze for at least 1 hour before serving.

Lavender Coconut Ice Cream

Lavender is a bit unusual for desserts, but it has a nice flowery flavor which is very strong so it should be used in small quantities.

Servings: 2-4 dishes

Ingredients:
1 cup coconut milk

1 cup cream of coconut

2 tablespoons edible lavender

2/3 cup sugar

Directions:

1. Pour the coconut milk into a small saucepan and bring to a boil. Remove from heat and stir in the lavender.

2. Let it infuse for 30 minutes then strain and discard the lavender.

3. Stir in the coconut cream and sugar then pour this mixture into your ice cream maker.

4. Freeze according to manufacturer's instructions then transfer to an airtight container and store in the freezer for as long as it takes.

Hazelnut Ice Cream

Nutty, creamy and rich are the best words to describe this amazing ice cream. If you like nuts, this will be a delight in every spoonful.

Servings: 2-4 dishes

Ingredients:

2 cups almond milk

1 cup hazelnuts, toasted and chopped

2 tablespoons dark rum

1/2 cup brown sugar

Directions:

1. In a bowl, mix the almond milk with the brown sugar and dark rum then pour the mixture into your ice cream maker.

2. Churn according to manufacturer's instructions. When almost done, throw in the chopped hazelnuts. Serve immediately or store in the freezer in an airtight container until serving.

Coffee Ice Cream

Coffee makes an excellent ice cream because the aroma is not as strong as in a brewed coffee and it blends perfectly with the coconut and almond milk.

Servings: 4-6 dishes

Ingredients:

1 cup coconut milk

1 cup almond milk

1 cup cream of coconut

4 teaspoons instant coffee

1 teaspoon vanilla extract

Directions:

1. Mix all the ingredients in a bowl and pour the mixture into your ice cream maker.

2. Freeze according to manufacturer's instructions then transfer to an airtight container and store in the freezer for as long as desired.

Sweet Potato Pecan Ice Cream

Yes, sweet potatoes and pecans come together in this recipe to create an ice cream perfect for warming up your days in fall because it also uses a lot of spices to flavor it.

Servings: 2-4 dishes

Ingredients:
2 sweet potatoes, peeled, steamed and mashed
1 cup coconut milk
1/4 cup sugar
1 teaspoon vanilla extract
2/3 cup pecans, chopped
1 teaspoon cinnamon
1 teaspoon ground ginger

Directions:

1. In a bowl, combine the mashed potatoes with the coconut milk, sugar, cinnamon, ginger and vanilla.

2. Pour this mixture into an ice cream maker and churn according to the instructions provided by the manufacturer of your machine. When almost done, throw in the chopped pecans. Serve right away or store in the freezer in an airtight container.

Banana Walnut Ice Cream

Banana and walnuts work great together as they are both rich and can yield a delicious ice cream that will also be very nutritious and filling.

Servings: 2-4 dishes

Ingredients:

4 ripe bananas, sliced and frozen
4 tablespoons coconut cream
1/4 cup walnuts, toasted and chopped
2 tablespoons brown sugar
1 teaspoon vanilla extract

Directions:

1. Put the frozen bananas in a blender or food processor and pulse until smooth.

2. Transfer into a bowl and stir in the coconut cream, brown sugar, vanilla and walnuts. Freeze for 2 hours before serving.

Pear Almond Ice Cream

Although pears are delicate, they do have a mild aroma which gets stronger when cooked. So this ice cream tastes like fall and it's amazing.

Servings: 2-4 dishes

Ingredients:

2 pears

3 tablespoons brown sugar

1 teaspoon lemon juice

1 cup almond milk

1/2 cup coconut cream

1 teaspoon vanilla extract

Directions:

1. In a heavy skillet, melt the brown sugar then stir in the pears, peeled and cut into slices. Cook them for 5-10 minutes in the caramel, adding the lemon juice. Remove from heat and set aside to cool.

2. In a bowl, combine the almond milk with the coconut cream and vanilla extract then pour into an ice cream maker and freeze according to instructions. When almost done, mix in the caramelized pears.

3. Serve right away or store in an airtight container in the freezer.

Raspberry Ice Cream

Raspberries are some of the most flavorsome berries so any dessert that uses them is delicious. Plus, they also have a beautiful color so the ice cream will be rather pink.

Servings: 2-4 dishes

Ingredients:

2 cups coconut milk

1/2 cup sugar

1 teaspoon vanilla extract

1 1/2 cups fresh raspberries

Directions:

1. In a small bowl, smash the raspberries with a fork so that there are only small chunks left. Stir in the sugar, coconut milk and vanilla.

2. Pour this mixture into the container of your ice cream maker and freeze as stated in the instructions of your machine.

3. Serve immediately or store in the freezer until you are ready to tuck in.

Chocolate Marbled Ice Cream

You gotta love interesting designs when it comes to desserts and there are a few tricks to creating nice looking desserts, just like this ice cream.

Servings: 2-4 dishes

Ingredients:
2 cups coconut milk
1/2 cup cream of coconut
2 teaspoon vanilla extract
1/3 cup brown sugar
1/4 cup cocoa powder
1/2 cup almond milk

Directions:

1. In a small saucepan, combine the almond milk with the cocoa powder and bring to a boil.

2. Simmer on low heat for 5-10 minutes. Remove from heat and let it cool.

3. In another bowl, mix the coconut milk, cream of coconut, vanilla and sugar then freeze this mixture in your ice cream maker. When almost done, gradually pour in the cocoa sauce you made earlier. By doing so, the ice cream will be marbled. Serve right away or store in an airtight container in the freezer.

Almond Crunch Vanilla Ice Cream

The almond crunch creates a nice contrast to the creaminess of the ice cream so the final dessert is fun to make and fun to eat.

Servings: 2-4 dishes

Ingredients:

1/2 cup sliced almonds

1/2 cup brown sugar

- 3 cups coconut milk
- 4 Seeds from 1 vanilla pod 4 tablespoons raw honey

Directions:

1. In a bowl, mix the coconut milk with sugar and vanilla seeds.

2. Churn this mixture into your ice cream maker.

3. In a small pan, melt the brown sugar then stir in the almonds.

4. Pour the hot sugar onto baking paper in a pan and let it set and cool. When chilled, break into smaller pieces.

5. Serve scoops of ice cream sprinkled with almond crunch.

Wild Berry Ice Cream

Wild berries have an amazing aroma and taste and they elevate any dessert they are being used in. This ice cream is no exception with it strong flavor and amazing fragrance.

Servings: 2-4 dishes

Ingredients:

1 1/2 cups frozen wild berries
1 cup coconut cream
1 cup almond milk
1/2 cup sugar
1 teaspoon vanilla extract

Directions:

1. In a bowl, mix together the coconut cream with the almond milk, sugar and vanilla extract.

2. Pour this mixture into your ice cream maker and churn according to the instructions provided by the manufacturer. When almost done, mix in the wild berries.

3. Serve immediately or store in an airtight container in the freezer.

Mango Chocolate Chip Ice Cream

Mango, coconut and chocolate come together in this amazing recipe to create a creamy and outstanding ice cream that will awaken your taste buds with its intense aroma.

Servings: 2-4 dishes

Ingredients:

2 ripe mangoes
1 cup coconut milk
1/2 cup coconut cream
1/2 cup raw sugar
1/2 cup chocolate chips

Directions:

1. Place the mango flesh in a blender and puree until smooth. Stir in the sugar, coconut milk, coconut cream and chocolate chips then pour the mixture into your ice cream maker.

2. Churn according to your machine's instructions then serve immediately or store in the freezer in an airtight container.

Spiced Chocolate Ice Cream

Chocolate works great with spices and this recipe uses a lot of spice. Don't say no before you try it; I promise you will be impressed.

Servings: 2-4 dishes

Ingredients:
1 cup coconut milk
1 cup almond milk
1 tablespoon cornstarch
1/2 cup cocoa powder
1/2 teaspoon cinnamon powder
1/4 teaspoon ground cloves
1 pinch cayenne pepper
1 pinch of salt

Directions:

1. Mix the almond milk with the cornstarch, cocoa powder and salt and place over a low heat.

2. Cook for a few minutes until it starts to thicken then remove from heat and let it cool completely.

3. Stir in the coconut milk, cinnamon, ground cloves and pepper then pour the mixture into your ice cream maker.

4. Churn according to your machine's instructions. Serve immediately or store in an airtight container in the freezer.

www.ingramcontent.com/pod-product-compliance
Lightning Source LLC
Chambersburg PA
CBHW070919080526
44589CB00013B/1369